ROMEO AND JULIET

or
The Old "You-Know-I-Really-Love-You-But-My-Father-Really-Hates-You" Blues

Adapted from Shakespeare's play
by
NANCY LINEHAN CHARLES

Dramatic Publishing
Woodstock, Illinois • England • Australia • New Zealand

*** NOTICE ***

IMPORTANT BILLING AND CREDIT REQUIREMENTS

All producers of the play must give credit to the author of the play in all programs distributed in connection with performances of the play and in all instances in which the title of the play appears for purposes of advertising, publicizing or otherwise exploiting the play and/or a production. The name of the author must also appear on a separate line, on which no other name appears, immediately following the title, and must appear in size of type not less than fifty percent the size of the title type. Biographical information on the author, if included in the playbook, may be used in all programs. *In all programs this notice must appear:*

Produced by special arrangement with
THE DRAMATIC PUBLISHING COMPANY of Woodstock, Illinois

ROMEO AND JULIET

or

The Old "You-Know-I-Really-Love-You-But-My-Father-Really-Hates-You" Blues

A Play in One Act
For 4 Men, 4 Women, 21 either gender

CHARACTERS

<u>FEMALES</u>
Juliet
Nurse
Lady Capulet
Lady Montague

<u>MALES</u>
Romeo
Paris
Mr. Capulet
Mr. Montague

<u>EITHER GENDER</u>
3 Storytellers (Jessie, Nicky, Loren)
Friar Lawrence
Prince Escalus
Benvolio
Tybalt
Mercutio
Abram
Gregory

Sampson
Balthasar/Servant/Voice
Newsperson
Cameraperson
Two Assistants
Fighters (at least 6, but as many as you like—includes
    Abram, Gregory, Sampson)
Townspeople (go for it)

It is important to understand that a great number of the characters can be played either by girls or boys. Shakespearean names should not be changed; girls will be playing males as males.

Costumes for this show ought to be expressed basically in two colors: Red (Juliet's family, the Capulets) and Blue (Romeo's family, the Montagues).

ROMEO AND JULIET
or
The Old "You-Know-I-Really-Love-You-But-My-Father-Really-Hates-You" Blues

AT RISE: *Bare stage. Two groups of teenagers or pre-teens (the FIGHTERS) start walking aggressively toward each other. They should be on opposite sides of the room, if possible, one group dressed in red, the other in blue. They shout insults across the audience at one another.*

BLUE 1
Hey, you.

RED 1
Who you talkin' to?

BLUE 1
You. I'm talkin' to you.

RED 2
You yellin' at my man here?

BLUE 2
Yeah. That's what he's sayin'.

(This stuff can get as mindless as you like. You can ad lib forever. Finally, JESSIE, a storyteller, steps out from R. Her character name should actually be the name of the person who's cast—male or female. She speaks to the audience.)

JESSIE
Don't anybody panic. This isn't a real fight.

(NICKY [storyteller 2] steps out from L.)

NICKY
No. This is like...ya know...a virtual fight.

(LOREN [storyteller 3] steps out from R.)

LOREN
Trust me...if this were real, you'd see tons of grownups all over these guys.

JESSIE
No, but see...this is how Bill Shakespeare starts off a story about true love.

NICKY
Just to let ya know that hate's gonna do its best to rain on the parade.
This is how he says it.

(A roving NEWSPERSON with trench coat and microphone walks with purpose to center stage. There's a CAMERAMAN with her. TWO ASSISTANTS fix her hair.

She looks directly into camera. She speaks with appropriate gravity.)

NEWSPERSON
Two households, both alike in dignity
(In fair Verona, where we lay our scene),
From ancient grudge break to new mutiny...
Where civil blood makes civil hands unclean...

(The FIGHTERS get up to the stage and begin circling each other. The NEWSPERSON dons a pith helmet and moves with caution through the gang of FIGHTERS. She holds the mike up to a BLUE FIGHTER.)

NEWSPERSON
Can you tell our audience why you're angry?

(The FIGHTER questioned shrugs his shoulders ["I dunno"]. NEWSPERSON approaches a RED FIGHTER.)

NEWSPERSON
And you, sir. What is your reason for engaging in this street brawl?

RED FIGHTER *(with a Brooklyn accent)*
Hey, lady. We do what we're told. Our families tell us to hate, we hate. No questions. *(He grabs the mike from her, looks at the camera and says:)* Details at eleven.

(All FIGHTERS laugh at his joke, then immediately go back to snarling at one another.)

JESSIE
OK. Just hold it a sec. Rewind the tape. Wha'd you just say?

(If the FIGHTERS can, they make movements as though they're going backwards. So does the NEWSPERSON. If someone can make a rewind sound, that's even better.)

RED FIGHTER
Our families tell us to hate, we hate.

(All freeze.)

JESSIE *(to the audience)*
Ever hear anything sillier? Somebody's mad at somebody...

NICKY
Tells Uncle Morty to hate that person...

LOREN
And pretty soon, the whole clan is involved...

JESSIE
...and it goes on for years. Till, honestly, no one even remembers who stepped on whose toe first.

NICKY
The big guy, Billy Shakespeare, was so good at this. My science teacher would say he knew how to dissect the underbelly.

LOREN
Yeah. Like runaway ambition in Macbeth, or jealousy in Othello.

JESSIE
In this case, the two fighting families are Romeo's family—the Montagues...

(All three MONTAGUES [dressed in blue] step from backstage and bow.)

NICKY
And Juliet's family—the Capulets.

(All three CAPULETS [dressed in red] step from backstage and bow.)

NICKY
Yeah...thanks for the curtsy, guys. But ya might try being polite to your enemy.
Just look what happens when hate runs riot. Go on, guys. Do your worst.

(GREGORY to SAMPSON, [red fighters—Capulets], indicating the blue gang members [Montagues].)

GREGORY
...The house of MONTAGUE!!!!!

SAMPSON
Quarrel. I will back thee.

GREGORY
I will frown as I pass by, and let them take it as they list.

SAMPSON *(suddenly inspired)*
I will bite my thumb at them, which is disgrace to them if they bear it.

JESSIE *(to audience)*
Oh, brother! He's saying biting your thumb at someone is the same as insulting them.

NICKY
Well...some things never change. Even today, people get upset over some stupid sign. Aren't people silly????

JESSIE
And by the way. Don't anybody get crazy over there being girl fighters. In this production, it's kinda cross-gender.

LOREN
I mean, in Shakespeare's day, men played ALL the parts. Women weren't allowed.

JESSIE
So it's payback time. Girls are playin' some guy parts. Chill.

(SAMPSON bites his thumb in the direction of the MONTAGUE GANG.)

ABRAM (blue) *(deeply offended)*
Do you bite your thumb at us, sir?

SAMPSON (red)
I do bite my thumb, sir.

ABRAM
Do you bite your thumb AT US, sir?

SAMPSON *(aside to GREGORY)*
Is the law of our side if I say "Ay"?

NICKY
Fighting is exhausting, isn't it? 'Cause, of course, nobody wants to get into trouble over it.

GREGORY
No.

SAMPSON *(to the MONTAGUES)*
No, sir. I do not bite my thumb at you, sir, but I bite my thumb, sir.

(They confer with their own gang members as to what to do. They form two huddles. They whisper loudly. Periodically one head pops up to look at the other gang. Finally...)

GREGORY (red)
Do you quarrel, sir?

ABRAM (blue)
Quarrel, sir? No, sir.

SAMPSON (red)
Draw if you be men.

   (They draw knives. BENVOLIO enters, dressed in blue.)

BENVOLIO
Part, fools!

JESSIE
This is Benvolio...Romeo's cousin.

BENVOLIO *(drawing his sword)*
Put up your swords. You know not what you do.

   (TYBALT enters, dressed in red, drawing HIS sword.)

TYBALT
Turn thee, Benvolio.

LOREN
This is Tybalt, Juliet's cousin. They call him the King of
Cats. Cool name, huh?

TYBALT
Look upon thy death.

BENVOLIO
I do but keep the peace. Put up thy sword,
Or manage it to part these men with me.

TYBALT
What, drawn and talk of peace? I hate the word
As I hate hell, all Montagues, and thee.

(They fight. The NEWSPERSON stands center and finishes her newscast.)

NEWSPERSON
From forth the fatal loins of these two foes
A pair of star-crossed lovers take their life.
(She turns to the CAMERAPERSON.)
How's my hair?

CAMERAPERSON
Perfect.

NEWSPERSON
That's a wrap. LUNCH!!!

(The NEWS TEAM runs off, as the FIGHTERS brawl. People come from everywhere shouting "Down With the Montagues; Down With the Capulets!!")

NICKY *(like a scolding parent)*
Oh great!!! Now the whole town's awake.

(MR. MONTAGUE and MR. CAPULET run in with their wives. Each family wears its color. The men are both old and have huge, outdated swords. They try to fight each other but weary of it very fast.)

JESSIE
So here we have Mr. Montague and Mr. Capulet...the guys who started the whole fight, YEARS ago, who are WAAAAY too old to be doing this sort of thing.

(From the back of the theatre, someone shouts.)

VOICE
Prince Escalus!!!!!

(Everybody screeches to a halt, looks to the back of the house, and gasps.)

LOREN
Here's the big cheese in this town—a PRINCE awready—and he's HAD it with this brawling. All rise, please. Bow your heads as the Prince comes by. Ladies? A slight curtsy would not be out of the question.

(She demonstrates the curtsy. The audience gets to its feet. If they don't, the STORYTELLERS need to force them by prodding. PRINCE ESCALUS comes from the back of the house to the stage. All the FIGHTERS stop and go down on one knee when they see him coming.)

PRINCE ESCALUS
Rebellious subjects, enemies to peace.
Three civil brawls
Have thrice disturbed the quiet of our streets...
If EVER you disturb our streets again,
Your lives shall pay the forfeit of the peace.
Once more, on pain of death, all men depart.

(Everyone starts to skulk away to offstage. The PRINCE goes back up the aisle.)

LOREN
He can do it too. He's the ruler and what he says, goes. Ya know, here we get to vote on stuff. Not in Verona!

(The MONTAGUES and BENVOLIO have remained behind.)

MONTAGUE *(to BENVOLIO)*
Who set this ancient quarrel?

LADY MONTAGUE *(to BENVOLIO)*
O, where is Romeo? Saw you him today?
Right glad I am he was not at this fray.

(ROMEO is seen, upstage, wearing blue, walking sadly.)

BENVOLIO
See where he comes. So please you, step aside.
I know his grievance.

MONTAGUE
Come, Madam, let's away.

(The MONTAGUES exit.)

BENVOLIO
Good morrow, cousin.

(He goes into conference with ROMEO.)

JESSIE
OK, see, Romeo has been moping around a lot lately and his cousin wants to know what's the deal? Turns out... well, I know this play is called *Romeo and Juliet*, but he hasn't met her yet and at the moment, he's head over heels in love with someone named Rosaline.

LOREN
Teenagers. My sister is just like that. Emotions are all over the place. Can anyone relate?

BENVOLIO
Tell me in sadness, who is that you love?

ROMEO
She hath forsworn to love.

NICKY
I guess Rosaline won't be his girlfriend.

BENVOLIO
Be ruled by me. Forget to think of her.

ROMEO *(desperately)*
O, teach me how I should forget to think.

BENVOLIO
By giving liberty unto thine eyes.
Examine other beauties.

ROMEO
Farewell. Thou canst not teach me to forget.

(ROMEO races out with BENVOLIO in pursuit. MR. CAPULET comes on with COUNTY PARIS.)

NICKY
The plot thickens. Here comes Juliet's father, with a guy who wants to marry Juliet. Boy!! They married 'em off early back then. How old is Juliet?

(JULIET walks onto the stage. She curtsies to the audience.)

JESSIE
How old would you say? Fourteen? Fifteen? *(The audience yells out ages.)* If ya said thirteen, you'd be right.

PARIS
Now, my lord, what say you to my suit?

CAPULET
My child hath not seen the change of fourteen years.

LOREN
See?

CAPULET
Let two more summers wither in their pride
Ere we may think her ripe to be a bride.

JESSIE
Oh, yeah. Let her marry at the ripe old age of fifteen. But back then, ya know, girls didn't go to college or work at Starbucks or anything.

LOREN
We've come a long way, baby.

PARIS
Younger than she are happy mothers made.

NICKY
Today we'd call that "children having children." But remember, this is olden times.

CAPULET
Woo her, gentle Paris, get her heart.
This night I hold an old accustomed feast
Whereto I have invited many a guest
Such as I love; and you among the store,
One more, most welcome, makes my number more.
(To a SERVANT.) Go, sir, find those persons
Whose names are written here.

*(He hands the SERVANT a long scroll. CAPULET
leaves, talking to PARIS. The SERVANT goes through the
audience, softly calling out names: Di Niro, Sinatra,
Nostradamus, Romano, Linguini, Chicken Cacciatori,
etc. [If there are actors in the play or in the community
with Italian surnames, it would be fun to put their last
names into this list].)*

NICKY
So, it's party time at the Capulets!! Romeo better get a
move on or Paris is gonna win the prize.

(Enter ROMEO and BENVOLIO. CAPULET's SERVANT approaches them with his party list.)

SERVANT
I pray you, sir, can you read?

ROMEO *(winking at BENVOLIO)*
Ay, if I know the letters and the language.

(ROMEO grabs the list and begins to read to himself. BENVOLIO looks over ROMEO's shoulder.)

ROMEO
A fair assembly. Whither should they come?

SERVANT
My master's...the great, rich Capulet, and, if you be not of the house of Montague, I pray come and crush a cup of wine.

(The SERVANT grabs his list and exits.)

BENVOLIO
At this same ancient feast of Capulet's
Sups the fair Rosaline whom thou so loves...

JESSIE
Uh-oh. They're gonna crash the party.

BENVOLIO
Compare her face with some that I shall show,
And I will make thee think thy swan a crow.

ROMEO
One fairer than my love? The all-seeing sun
Ne'er saw her match since first the world began.

BENVOLIO
Tut...

JESSIE
Tut. I like that word, tut. Kinda like...NOT!!!

BENVOLIO
Tut, you saw her fair, none else being by.

ROMEO
I'll go along.

(They exit.)

NICKY
So...Romeo and his Montague pals are going in disguise to
a party at the Capulets.

JESSIE
Sounds like trouble to me. Not to mention Juliet's parents
are fattening her up for the kill.

NICKY
Gussying her up to meet Paris: the guy THEY want her to
marry.

JESSIE
AT THIRTEEN. REMEMBER???

NICKY
Yup. Paris will be at the party at her father's invitation. Things are movin' fast. Come on, Romeo.

LOREN
Just so you know, the girl had very little to say about it.

NICKY
Yeah. If she didn't totally, like, throw up when she met him, and he had a lot of money and land and stuff...

JESSIE
...well, it was sort of a done deal.

(We hear a piercing yell from the back of the house. LADY CAPULET is a bit of a narcissist...spoiled and loud [a deadly combo]. She barrels down the aisle, with the NURSE trailing behind her.)

LADY CAPULET
NURSE!!!! Where's my daughter????? Call her forth to me!

(The NURSE knows her place as a servant, but is definitely on JULIET's side in everything. The trick for her is to maneuver around LADY CAPULET to accomplish what JULIET wants.)

NURSE
I bade her come. *(Calling.)* Lamb...ladybird...what, Juliet.

(JULIET enters.)

JULIET
How now, who calls?

NURSE *(raising her eyebrows in warning to JULIET)*
Your mother.

JULIET
Madam, I am here. What is your will?

LADY C
Nurse, thou knowest my daughter's
Of a pretty age.

NURSE *(flatly)*
She's not fourteen.

LADY C
I pray thee, hold thy peace.

NURSE
Peace. I have done.

> *(But she continues to make faces behind LADY CAPU-*
> *LET's back. The NURSE is not for this marriage.)*

LADY C
Tell me, daughter Juliet,
How stands your disposition to be married?

JULIET
It is an honor that I dream not of.

LADY C *(warning her)*
Well, think of marriage now.
The valiant Paris seeks you for his love.

NURSE *(exploding)*
Why, he's a man of wax!!!!!

LADY C *(glaring at the NURSE)*
Verona's summer hath not such a flower.
(To JULIET.) What say you?
Can you love the gentleman?
This night you shall behold him at our feast.

*(She looks expectantly at JULIET. JULIET looks less
than enthusiastic. This enrages LADY C. She barks at
her daughter.)*

LADY C
Speak briefly. Can you like of Paris' love?

JULIET *(intimidated by her mother's rage)*
I'll look to like.

(The SERVANT comes in.)

SERVANT
Madam, the guests are come.

LADY C
We follow thee. Juliet? The County stays.

LOREN
She means, "Come along, girlie. Paris is waiting." See they
sometimes call Paris, "the County," 'cause he's a count.
County—Count. See how that works?

*(As JULIET stands immobile, the NURSE gently pushes
her after her mother.)*

NURSE
Go, girl.

(They exit.)

JESSIE
Don't'cha like the way she says "Go, girl"? Sassy...just
like us modern girls. GO, GIRLFRIEND!!!!

NICKY
So...we're fifteen minutes into this play and Romeo and
Juliet HAVEN'T EVEN MET. And last we heard...Romeo
was pining away for someone named Rosaline.

LOREN
Well, we don't have all night. Let's get on with it. A little
cocktail conversation, please. Talk amongst yourselves.

JESSIE *(to the audience)*
Go on...we're not kidding...talk to your neighbor. We'll
tell you when to stop.

*(PARTYERS run onto the stage with decorations, shout-
ing and jumping about. They perform a little dance. RO-*

*MEO, MERCUTIO, BENVOLIO and all their friends
[THREE OR FOUR GUYS, all dressed in blue] enter.
They are all wearing masks.)*

NICKY *(to the audience)*
All right. That'll do. Enough, already. Finally Romeo is
within shouting distance of Juliet. Listen up.

*(JESSIE and NICKY run to DC and hold their arms up
as if they form a doorway. The GUYS pause there.)*

ROMEO
Under love's heavy burden do I sink.

MERCUTIO
If love be rough with you, be rough with love.

BENVOLIO
Come. Knock and enter.

*(ROMEO knocks, the TWO STORYTELLERS move their
arms as though ushering the YOUNG MEN through the
door. All go but ROMEO, MERCUTIO and BENVOLIO.
ROMEO sits dejected. The THREE remove their masks.
The STORYTELLERS look at their watches impatiently,
and make gestures for ROMEO to get the heck inside
and meet JULIET.)*

ROMEO *(dejected)*
I dreamt a dream tonight.

(The STORYTELLERS roll their eyes heavenward, plop down where they are, and put their heads in their hands.)

MERCUTIO
Dreamers often lie.

ROMEO
In bed asleep...they do dream things true.

MERCUTIO
O. Then I see Queen Mab hath been with you.
She is the fairies' midwife.
Her chariot is an empty hazelnut.
She gallops night by night
Through lovers' brains, and then they dream of love.
Sometime she driveth o'er a soldier's neck,
And then he dreams of cutting foreign throats...
Drums in his ear, at which he starts and wakes
And being thus frighted, swears a prayer or two
And sleeps again.

(ROMEO cuts him off.)

ROMEO
Peace, peace, Mercutio, peace.
Thou talk'st of nothing.

MERCUTIO
True, I talk of dreams,
Which are the children of an idle brain,
And more inconstant than the wind.

BENVOLIO
This wind you talk of blows us from ourselves.
Supper is done and we shall come too late.

(The STORYTELLERS jump up expectantly: are the boys FINALLY going to the party?)

ROMEO
On, lusty gentlemen.

BENVOLIO
Strike, drum.

(We hear reveling music but a fateful drum keeping time. The three BOYS put on their masks, and march around the stage, ROMEO held up by his two friends, who continue to try and cheer him up. All the partyers come on; they spill out into the audience and throw glitter over the crowd. Music is being played. The three STORY-TELLERS assume positions like statues in a garden. Periodically, they talk to the audience, but still maintain their statue positions. JULIET is dancing with PARIS. ROMEO sees her. He stops dead and stares. He hides behind one of the statues. He removes his mask.)

ROMEO
What lady's that which doth enrich the hand
Of yonder Knight?
O, she doth teach the torches to burn bright!
Did my heart love till now? Forswear it, sight,
For I n'er saw true beauty till this night.

JESSIE *(the statue he's hiding behind. To the audience)*
Anybody remember the name "Rosaline"? The good news
is, he's FINALLY seen Juliet. And now...nothing else mat-
ters.

*(Indeed, ROMEO and JULIET are looking pie-eyed at
each other.)*

NICKY
I believe this is what's known as "love at first sight."

*(The dance ends and PARIS turns away from JULIET to
talk to someone. ROMEO comes up behind her and
takes her hand.)*

ROMEO *(taking JULIET's hand)*
If I profane with my unworthiest hand
This holy shrine, the gentle sin is this:
My lips, two blushing pilgrims, ready stand
To smooth that rough touch with a tender kiss.

JULIET
Good pilgrim, you do wrong your hand too much,
For saints have hands that pilgrims' hands do touch.

ROMEO
Have not saints lips?

JULIET
Ay, pilgrim.

ROMEO
O then, dear saint, let lips do what hands do.
(He kisses her hand.)

JESSIE
Fast worker, no? But here comes nursie. Mama calls.

NURSE *(to JULIET)*
Your mother craves a word with you.

(JULIET moves toward her mother.)

ROMEO *(to the NURSE)*
What is her mother? (Note: "What" means "Who")

NURSE
Her mother is the lady of the house.

(The NURSE moves away.)

ROMEO *(to himself—in despair)*
Is she a Capulet? Ay, so I fear.

BENVOLIO
Away, begone.

(All start to leave. ROMEO's FRIENDS are dragging him...his eyes are on JULIET. She and the NURSE are leaving but her eyes are on ROMEO.)

JULIET
Come hither, Nurse.
What's he that follows here that would not dance?

NURSE
I know not.

JULIET
Go ask his name.

(The NURSE goes to ROMEO.)

JULIET
If he be married,
My grave is like to be my wedding bed.

NICKY
Yikes! She's saying if she can't have him, she'll never
marry ANYONE. Harsh!

JESSIE
But then remember: She's an emotional teenager. Only
THIRTEEN!!!!

NURSE *(returning)*
His name is Romeo, and a Montague,
The only son of your great enemy.

JULIET *(horrified)*
My only love sprung from my only hate!
That I must love a loathed enemy!

NURSE
Let's away.

(All exit, but ROMEO lingers. His friends have to keep coming back after him.)

NICKY
All right, well, see, here's a big old problem. These two thirteen-year-olds have *seen* each other for, oh maybe a minute.

LOREN
Yet they're drawn to each other immediately...

NICKY
...but when they hear each other's names...

LOREN
...*right away*...they have to remember that old hate between their parents.

JESSIE
Stupid. *(To the audience.)* Let's all say "BOO" to holding old grudges.

(The STORYTELLERS prod the audience until they comply and everyone is shouting "Boo.")

ROMEO
Can I go forward when my heart is here?

(There is a decorative ladder representing the wall around JULIET's house. ROMEO climbs it, over the top, and down into the CAPULET garden. He sneaks around the garden, trying to find JULIET's window. The STORYTELLERS wheel her on. She's at the top of a ladder, looking lovesick.)

JESSIE
So basically, here's the picture. Romeo has forgotten completely about Rosaline and has fallen in love with the daughter of his family's enemy.

LOREN
He's sneaked into her garden, where...

NICKY
...if he's caught...

JESSIE *(draws her finger across her throat and makes the throat-cutting sound)*
Does the thought of that...slow down this teenage lover?????

LOREN
Not a chance!!!

(The STORYTELLERS retire to the side.)

ROMEO
But soft, what light through yonder window breaks?
It is the East, and Juliet is the sun.
Arise, fair sun, and kill the envious moon,

Who is already sick and pale with grief
That thou, her maid, art far more fair than she.

(*JULIET doesn't see or hear ROMEO. He pushes himself up flush against her ladder. She speaks to the
moon.*)

JULIET
Ay me.

ROMEO *(whispering)*
She speaks.
O, speak again, bright angel.

JULIET
O Romeo, Romeo, wherefore art thou, Romeo?
Deny thy father and refuse thy name,
Or, if thou wilt not, be but sworn my love,
And I'll no longer be a Capulet.

ROMEO *(amazed)*
Shall I hear more, or shall I speak at this?

JULIET
'Tis but thy name that is my enemy.
What's "Montague"? O, be some other name!
What's in a name? That which we call a rose
By any other word would smell as sweet.
Romeo, doff thy name,
And, for thy name, which is no part of thee,
Take all myself.

(ROMEO springs out of his hiding place. JULIET nearly falls off her ladder.)

JESSIE
Smooth.

ROMEO
I take thee at thy word.
Call me but love, and I'll be new baptized.
Henceforth I never will be Romeo.

JULIET *(frightened)*
What man art thou?

ROMEO
My name, dear saint, is hateful to myself
Because it is an enemy to thee.

JULIET
Art thou not Romeo, and a Montague?

ROMEO
Neither, fair maid, if either thee dislike.

JULIET
How camest thou hither, tell me, and wherefore?
The orchard walls are high and hard to climb,
And the place death, considering who thou art.

ROMEO
Thy kinsmen are no stop to me.

JULIET
If they do see thee, they will murder thee.

ROMEO
I have night's cloak to hide me from their eyes.

JULIET *(blurting out)*
Dost thou love me?
O gentle Romeo,
If thou dost love, pronounce it faithfully.

ROMEO *(sincerely)*
Lady, by yonder blessed moon I vow...

JULIET *(quickly)*
O, swear not by the moon, th' inconstant moon...

ROMEO
What shall I swear by?

JULIET
Well, do not swear. Although I joy in thee,
I have no joy of this contract tonight.
It is too rash, too unadvised, too sudden.
Good night, good night.

ROMEO
O, wilt thou leave me so unsatisfied?

JULIET *(pointedly)*
What satisfaction canst thou have tonight?

ROMEO
Th' exchange of thy love's faithful vow for mine.

(The NURSE calls from offstage.)

JULIET
Three words, dear Romeo, and good night indeed.
If that thy bent of love be honorable,
Thy purpose marriage,
Send me word tomorrow,
By one that I'll procure to come to thee...

NICKY
A messenger!!!!!!

NURSE *(from within)*
Madam.

JULIET *(shouting to the NURSE)*
I come anon.
(To ROMEO.) But if thou meanest not well,
I do beseech thee—

NURSE *(within)*
Madam.

JULIET *(shouting to the NURSE)*
By and by I come.
(To ROMEO.) I do beseech thee
To cease thy strife and leave me to my grief.
Tomorrow will I send.

(The STORYTELLERS start to wheel her ladder off. Here begins a series of [what should be] comical entrances and exits.)

ROMEO
So thrive my soul...

JULIET *(as they wheel her away, she blows a kiss to him)*
My Romeo!!

ROMEO
It is my soul that calls upon my name.

JULIET *(breathlessly)*
Romeo.

(STORYTELLERS stop wheeling her off.)

ROMEO
My dear.

JULIET *(gazes at him. Forgot what she was going to say. Remembering)*
What o'clock tomorrow
Shall I send to thee.

ROMEO *(gazing longingly at her)*
By the hour of nine.

JULIET
I will not fail.

(They gaze, moon-eyed, in silence.)

JULIET
'Tis twenty year till then.

(Silence. STORYTELLERS look at their watches, clear their throats, tap their feet.)

JULIET
I have forgot why I did call thee back.

ROMEO
Let me stand here till thou remember it.

JESSIE
Oh, please. (Note: that's "puh-leeze")

JULIET
I shall forget to have thee stand there,
Rememb'ring how I love thy company.

ROMEO
And I'll still stay, to have thee still forget.

NICKY
Lovers say the dumbest things, don't they.

(JULIET hears something within. Jumps. STORY-TELLERS start to wheel her off again.)

JULIET
Good night, good night. Parting is such sweet sorrow.

(ROMEO and JULIET throw kisses to each other.)

ROMEO
Hence will I to my ghostly friar's cell,
His help to crave, and my dear hap to tell.

(He runs offstage, through the audience, if possible. If not, this just takes place onstage. Finds FRIAR LAW-RENCE. Brings him down the other aisle, confiding in him all the way. The STORYTELLERS have finished wheeling JULIET off and come downstage. The two stop and FRIAR LAWRENCE shakes a finger at ROMEO.)

FRIAR LAWRENCE
Holy Saint Francis, what a change is here.
Is Rosaline, that thou didst love so dear,
So soon forsaken?

ROMEO
Thou chid'st me oft for loving Rosaline.

FRIAR LAWRENCE *(protesting)*
For DOTING, not for loving, pupil mine.

ROMEO
I pray thee, chide me not.

(The two go off in conference, L.)

LOREN
But the good friar agrees to help him out.

JESSIE
The friar believes that maybe the two families would stop fighting if the kids got together. Sounds good on paper.

(ROMEO leaves FRIAR LAWRENCE L. Starts to cross to R. He's in a hurry. BENVOLIO and MERCUTIO enter. They see ROMEO and yell. They begin teasing their friend.)

MERCUTIO
Signior Romeo, bonjour. You gave us the counterfeit last night.

ROMEO
What counterfeit did I give you?

MERCUTIO
The slip, sir. The slip.

ROMEO *(trying to get away)*
Pardon, good Mercutio, my business was great, and in such a case as mine a man may strain courtesy.

(The NURSE enters. She approaches MERCUTIO and BENVOLIO.)

NURSE
Gentlemen, can any of you tell me where I may find the young Romeo?

JESSIE
OK. Here's Juliet's messenger to find out if Romeo's for real about marriage.

NICKY
Or just a lotta talk.

LOREN
Hot air.

JESSIE
Baloney.

NICKY
You know the kind.

ROMEO *(excited)*
I am the youngest of that name.

NURSE
If you be he, sir, I desire some confidence with you.

(She pushes him with force. MERCUTIO and BENVOLIO giggle.)

MERCUTIO & BENVOLIO
Romeo, will you come to your father's? We'll to dinner thither.

ROMEO
I will follow you.

(They run off laughing. The NURSE is angry.)

NURSE
I pray you, sir, what saucy merchant was this?

ROMEO *(eager to hear the message from JULIET)*
A gentleman, Nurse, that loves to hear himself talk.

NURSE
An he speak anything against me, I'll take him down.

JESSIE
She can do it too.

NURSE
I am so vexed that every part about me quivers. Scurvy knave!

JESSIE
Ooooh. I like the sound of that: "Scurvy Knave." I plan to incorporate that into my English vocabulary word list. Scurvy Knave.

LOREN
There are lots of Scurvy Knaves in my science class. I think we're gonna dissect some.

(ROMEO takes the NURSE by the shoulders and turns her away from where MERCUTIO and BENVOLIO were. He walks her around the stage. She stops.)

NURSE
If you should lead her in a fool's paradise, as they say, it were a very gross kind of behavior, as they say.

ROMEO
Commend me to thy lady and mistress. Bid her devise
Some means to come to shrift this afternoon,
And there she shall at Friar Lawrence's cell
Be shrived and married.

JESSIE
Wastes no time, this one...

NICKY
"Shrift" means confession before a priest. "Shrived" means being forgiven by the priest. For the non-Romans among us.

NURSE
This afternoon, sir? Well, she shall be there.

(The NURSE leaves joyously with her servant. ROMEO runs off. JULIET paces on, wringing her hands, waiting for the NURSE.)

JULIET
The clock struck nine when I did send the nurse.
In half an hour she promised to return.
(She hears something.) Oh, God, she comes.

(The NURSE enters.)

JULIET
O, honey Nurse, what news?
Hast thou met with him?

NURSE
I am aweary. Give me leave awhile.
Fie, how my bones ache! What a jaunt have I!

JULIET *(losing patience)*
I would thou hadst my bones, and I thy news.
Nay, come, I pray thee, speak. Good, good Nurse,
speak.

NURSE
Jesu, what haste! Can you not stay awhile?
Do you not see that I am out of breath?

JULIET
How art thou out of breath, when thou hast breath
To say to me that thou art out of breath?
Is thy news good or bad?
Let me be satisfied; is it good or bad?

NURSE
Romeo? He is not the flower of courtesy,
But I'll warrant him as gentle as a lamb.

JULIET
But all this I did know before.
What says he of our marriage? What of that?

NURSE
Lord, how my head aches! What a head have I?

JULIET
I AM SORRY THAT THOU ART NOT WELL!!!
Sweet, sweet, sweet Nurse, tell me, what says my love?

NURSE
Your love says, like an honest gentleman, and a courteous,
and a kind, and a handsome, and, I warrant, a virtuous—
Where is your mother?

JULIET
Where is my mother? Why, she is within.
Where should she be? How oddly thou repliest:
"Your love says like an honest gentleman,
Where is your mother?"

NURSE
Henceforward do your messages yourself.

JULIET *(pleading)*
WHAT—SAYS—ROMEO??????

NURSE *(conspiratorially)*
Have you got leave to go to shrift today?

JULIET
I have.

NURSE
Then hie you hence to Friar Lawrence's cell.
There stays a husband to make you a wife.

(JULIET begins leaping for joy.)

NURSE
Now comes the wanton blood up in your cheeks.
Go. I'll to dinner. Hie you to the cell.

(JULIET is laughing and dancing all the way offstage.)

LOREN
Boy, love can make ya silly, huh. So. She's pretending to
go to mass and confession, but really she's going to marry
Romeo in Friar Lawrence's cell.

NICKY
Mom and Dad'll find this hard to swallow...even with dinner.

JESSIE
Which is why she's not telling Mom and Dad...who are
still laboring under the delusion that she's gonna marry
Paris!!!!

LOREN
But so much is the theatre magical and swift, we can tell
you right now...

(All three STORYTELLERS snap their fingers.)

NICKY
She's ALREADY married Romeo. Offstage, don't'cha know.

JESSIE
Now, Romeo, the new groom, is gonna sneak in to see Juliet, the new bride...

JESSIE
But on the way...who does he run into but Tybalt...

NICKY
...Juliet's cousin...

JESSIE
...fighting with Romeo's best friend, Mercutio.

LOREN
And remember: Romeo has just become Tybalt's COUSIN, through marriage to Juliet. He doesn't WANT this fight.

(We see the MONTAGUE gang fighting with the CAP-ULET gang. Here's a chance for a good Westside Story fight—with swords, if ya got 'em. ROMEO tries to separate them.)

TYBALT *(to ROMEO)*
Thou art a villain.

ROMEO
Villain am I none.
Therefore farewell. I see thou knowest me not.

TYBALT
Turn and draw!!!!

ROMEO
I do protest I never injured thee
But love thee better than thou canst devise
Till thou shalt know the reason of my love.
And so, good Capulet, which name I tender
As dearly as my own, be satisfied.

(The FIGHTERS freeze. LOREN steps forward.)

LOREN
This would not be the "manly" thing to say.

MERCUTIO (exploding at ROMEO)
O calm, dishonorable, vile submission!!

LOREN
Wha'd I tell you?

MERCUTIO (draws his sword)
Tybalt, you ratcatcher, will you walk?

TYBALT
What would'st thou have with me?

MERCUTIO
Good King of Cats, nothing but one of your nine lives.

TYBALT
I am for you!
(He draws his sword.)

ROMEO
Gentle Mercutio, put thy rapier up.

MERCUTIO *(to TYBALT)*
Come, sir.

*(They begin to fight. Again, a chance for some great
swordplay.)*

JESSIE
Now Romeo's *gotta* fight to STOP the fight.

ROMEO *(drawing his sword)*
Draw, Benvolio, beat down their weapons.
Hold, Tybalt! Good, Mercutio!!

(TYBALT stabs MERCUTIO. MERCUTIO staggers.)

ABRAM
Away, Tybalt!

(The MONTAGUES run offstage.)

MERCUTIO
I am hurt. A plague on both your houses.

BENVOLIO
What, art thou hurt?

MERCUTIO
Ay, ay, a scratch, a scratch. Marry, 'tis enough.

ROMEO
Courage, man, the hurt cannot be much.

MERCUTIO
No, 'tis not so deep as a well, nor so wide as a church door, but 'tis enough. 'Twill serve. Ask for me tomorrow, and you shall find me a grave man. A plague on both your houses! *(To ROMEO.)* Why the devil came you between us?

ROMEO
I thought all for the best.

MERCUTIO
Help me into some house, Benvolio,
Or I shall faint. A plague on both your houses.

(BENVOLIO helps MERCUTIO off.)

ROMEO
My very friend hath got this mortal hurt
In my behalf. O sweet Juliet,
Thy beauty hath made me effeminate.

(BENVOLIO runs in.)

BENVOLIO
Oh, Romeo, Romeo, brave Mercutio's dead.

(ROMEO is stunned. TYBALT enters again.)

ROMEO *(enraged)*
Alive in triumph, and Mercutio slain!
Now, Tybalt, take the "villain" back again
That late thou gavest me, for Mercutio's soul
Is but a little way above our heads,
Staying for thine to keep him company.
Either thou or I, or both, must go with him.

(They fight. ROMEO stabs TYBALT, who falls and dies. Everyone freezes.)

NICKY
Ya see how these things happen. No one can stop playing out the grudge. They always think the other guy should stop first.

(The actors break the freeze.)

BENVOLIO
Romeo, away, begone! The Prince will doom thee death
If thou art taken.

ROMEO *(screaming)*
O, I am Fortune's fool!

(ROMEO flees. The PRINCE and TOWNSPEOPLE enter—including MR. and MRS. CAPULET and MR. and MRS. MONTAGUE.)

PRINCE
Where are the vile beginners of this fray?

BENVOLIO
O, noble Prince,
There lies the man, slain by young Romeo,
That slew brave Mercutio.

LADY CAPULET *(weeping)*
Tybalt, my cousin, O my brother's child!

JESSIE
Juliet's mother. Tybalt was her nephew. Sad.

LADY CAPULET
O, Prince!
For blood of ours, shed blood of Montague!

PRINCE
Benvolio, who began this bloody fray?

BENVOLIO
Tybalt, here slain, who Romeo's hand did slay.

LADY CAPULET *(hysterically)*
Romeo slew Tybalt; Romeo must not live!

PRINCE
Romeo slew him; he slew Mercutio.
For Romeo's offence,
Immediately do we exile him hence.
I will be deaf to pleading and excuses.
Therefore use none.

(The PRINCE exits with the TOWNSPEOPLE. ROMEO's MOTHER breaks down crying. She is led away.)

NICKY
Told you he was tough.

LOREN
So there it is. The Prince thinks he's being kind, not *killing* Romeo for brawling and killing Tybalt. He's just exiling him instead.

JESSIE
For those of you unfamiliar with the word "exile"? It's like detention for the rest of your life.

LOREN
Without the laughs.

NICKY
But well...whatever...Juliet hasn't heard about any of this. She's still waiting in her room for Romeo—HER HUS-BAND—to come see her.

LOREN
She's BEGGING the sun to go down because Romeo is coming to see her at night.

(JULIET enters and is nervous and excited.)

JULIET
Gallop apace, you fiery-footed steeds.
If love be blind, it best agrees with night.

Come, night; come, Romeo;
For thou wilt lie upon the wings of night
Whiter than new snow upon a raven's back.
Give me my Romeo; and, when he shall die,
Take him and cut him out in little stars,
And he will make the face of heaven so fine
That all the world will be in love with night
And pay no worship to the garish sun.

(The NURSE bursts in, wringing her hands.)

JULIET
Ay me! What news? Why dost thou wring thy hands?

NURSE
Tybalt is gone and Romeo banish-ed.
Romeo that killed him, he is banish-ed.

JULIET
O God! Did Romeo's hand shed Tybalt's blood?

NURSE
It did, it did! alas the day, it did!
Shame come to Romeo!

JULIET
Blistered be thy tongue
For such a wish.

NURSE
Will you speak well of him that killed your cousin?

JULIET
Shall I speak ill of him that is my husband?
My husband lives, that Tybalt would have slain.
Yet some word there was, worser than Tybalt's death:
"Tybalt is dead and Romeo—banish-ed."
"Romeo is banish-ed"—
There is no end, no limit, measure, bound,
In that word's death.

NURSE
Hie to your chamber. I'll find Romeo
To comfort you.

JULIET
O find him,
And bid him come to take his last farewell.

(The NURSE exits.)

JESSIE
Well that'll throw a tub of cold water on your wedding
day, won't it?

NICKY
Yeah. Not only is your cousin dead, but your husband has
killed him and now has been ordered away for the rest of
his life.

LOREN
Well...moving right along...the nurse finds Romeo in Friar
Lawrence's cell. The friar tells Romeo to go on to Juliet's

room, say goodbye, hie-tail it to a town called Mantua (Man-chew-uh) and wait to hear from the friar.

JESSIE
He's got…a PLAN.

(We see the lovers wave to each other and blow kisses. Start to part, turn and blow more kisses. And more. And more.)

NICKY
You get the picture.

(Both lovers finally leave the stage.)

JESSIE
And right on the heels of that…enter Juliet's mama. With some reeeeeally interesting news.

LADY CAPULET
Early next Thursday morn
The County Paris, at St. Peter's Church
Shall happily make thee there a joyful bride.

(JULIET and the STORYTELLERS turn full front to the audience, open wide eyes, and drop their jaws.)

JULIET *(to her mother)*
I pray you tell my lord and father, madam,
I will not marry yet.

LADY CAPULET
Here comes your father. Tell him so yourself.

ALL THREE STORYTELLERS
UH-OH!!

CAPULET
How now, wife?
Have you delivered to her our decree?

LADY CAPULET
Ay, sir; but she will none, she gives you thanks.
I would the fool were married to her grave.

CAPULET *(enraged at JULIET)*
Get thee to church a Thursday
Or never after look me in the face.

JESSIE
YIKES!!!!! He's disowning her!!!

(JULIET, now in tears, throws herself at her father's feet, begging him to reconsider.)

CAPULET
Speak not, reply not, do not answer me!
My fingers itch.

(He raises his hand to slap her. The NURSE stops him.)

NURSE
May not one speak?

CAPULET
Peace, you mumbling fool.

CAPULET *(red with rage now. To JULIET)*
Thursday is near:
An you be mine, I'll give you to my friend;
And you be not, hang, beg, starve, die in the streets,
For by my soul, I'll ne'er acknowledge thee.

(CAPULET exits. JULIET tries to hug her mother. Her mother throws her off.)

LADY CAPULET
Talk not to me, for I'll not speak a word.
Do as thou wilt, for I have done with thee.

(LADY CAPULET exits. The NURSE helps JULIET off.)

JESSIE
Makes your own parents look pretty good, huh?

(We see JULIET conferring with FRIAR LAWRENCE.)

LOREN
So Juliet, races to Friar Lawrence to ask him what in the heck she should do, before she ends up with TWO husbands.

JESSIE
At THIRTEEN!!!! TWO...not ONE!!!! TWO!!!!

NICKY
But remember, Friar Lawrence is the MAN with the PLAN.

(FRIAR LAWRENCE pulls a medicine vial from his pocket.)

FRIAR LAWRENCE *(to JULIET)*
Tomorrow night...
Take thou this vial,
And this distilling liquid drink thou off.
When presently through all thy veins shall run
A cold and drowsy humor.
No warmth, no breath, shall testify thou livest.
Each part shall appear like death.

*(FRIAR LAWRENCE and JULIET walk around the stage
and he explains to her in mime.)*

LOREN
He tells her she'll look like she's dead for forty-eight hours.

JESSIE *(to the audience)*
DO NOT try this at home.

NICKY
Her parents will weep and wail...

JESSIE
...and wish they hadn't been so mean to her...

NICKY
Every kid's fantasy.

LOREN
They'll put her in the family tomb...the friar will contact
Romeo and tell him to sneak back to Verona and rescue his
love.

*(JULIET grabs the vial, hugs the FRIAR, dances off the
stage. The FRIAR begins writing a letter to ROMEO. A
group of mourners appears, carrying JULIET on their
shoulders, her parents weeping behind.)*

JESSIE
OK now. He means well. He thinks when the parents dis-
cover the trick, they'll be soooooo glad to have Juliet alive,
they won't care WHO she's married to.

*(The mourners lay her on the front of the stage. There's
one mourner [BALTHASAR] who runs offstage, down
the aisle.)*

LOREN
But see that guy? Name's "Balthasar." That one!!! Stop him!!

*(He gets to the back of the auditorium and grabs RO-
MEO. He takes him down the aisle as he talks to him.)*

NICKY
Yeah, well, he's the guy who throws a monkey wrench into
the friar's perfect plan.

JESSIE
Because he isn't with the program, see? He thinks Juliet is
REALLY dead.

BALTHASAR
I saw her laid low in her kindred's vault.

ROMEO
Is it even so??? Then I defy you, stars!
I will hence tonight.

(BALTHASAR leaves.)

ROMEO
Well, Juliet, I will lie with thee tonight.

JESSIE
Uh-oh. See here's the rub, as they say in Shakespeare. Everybody is now operating on half-truths. Ever play the game "Gossip"? This is not good.

LOREN
So Romeo heads for Verona...picks up a little poison along the way.

NICKY
OK, now THIS is the real thing. Not a fake—like Juliet's—that makes you LOOK dead. THIS stuff makes you BE dead.

(ROMEO runs offstage.)

JESSIE
Meanwhile, Friar Lawrence finds out his letter to Romeo didn't get to Romeo.

LOREN
No kidding. Snail mail. Sloooooooowwwwww. If they had had e-mail?... No tragedy. No play. You'd be home watchin' some reality show.

NICKY
But they didn't. So Friar Lawrence figures he needs to go to Juliet's tomb and help her when she wakes up.

JESSIE
'Cause, see, she'll be surrounded by dead ancestors in the family tomb. It's like, what if you weren't so crazy about Uncle Morty in LIFE...

LOREN
...you wouldn't wanna hang with him DEAD... would'ja???

NICKY
So the friar is on his way, but so is Romeo.

JESSIE
To hang with the gang of dead guys.

    (ROMEO approaches the "dead" JULIET.)

ROMEO
Here, here will I remain,
And shake the yoke of inauspicious stars
From this world-wearied flesh.
(He holds the vial of poison up.)
Here's to my love!
(He drinks. ROMEO dies.)

JESSIE
OK, well...there goes our hero. And all for a stupid fight that no one even remembers what it was about...

LOREN
Too late, of course, Friar Lawrence busts into the tomb.

NICKY
What is it with this guy? He's 0 for 3.

FRIAR LAWRENCE
Romeo! O, pale.
The lady stirs.

(*JULIET awakens.*)

JESSIE
So we still got a heroine with a pulse. Let's see if Lawrence can manage to keep HER alive.

JULIET
O comfortable Friar! Where is my lord?
Where is my Romeo?

FRIAR LAWRENCE
Come, come away.
Thy husband there lies dead;
Come, I'll dispose of thee
Among a sisterhood of holy nuns.

LOREN
So she's gonna go from almost TWO husbands to nuns.
How can she refuse?

JULIET *(fiercely)*
Go, get thee hence, for I will not away.

(The FRIAR runs away in fear. JULIET picks up the vial.)

JULIET
Poison, I see, hath been his timeless end.
(She tries to drink from the vial but finds no poison left.)
Drunk all? And left no friendly drop
To help me after?

(Voices are heard offstage approaching the tomb.)

JULIET
Noise? Then I'll be brief.
(She snatches ROMEO's dagger.)
O happy dagger!

*(JULIET stabs herself and dies. Everyone rushes on-
stage, the MONTAGUES and CAPULETS are weeping.
PRINCE ESCALUS looks over the dead bodies.)*

JESSIE
Oh, yeah, now that everyone's dead, everyone's crying.
Why is it people can't patch it up before there are dead
bodies all over the place? Can anyone tell me that????

PRINCE
Where be these enemies? Capulet, Montague,
See what a scourge is laid upon your hate?
All are punished.
For never was a story of more woe
Than this of Juliet and her Romeo.

(STORYTELLERS all come to the lip of the stage. They address the audience.)

JESSIE
So, hey. You got a bone to pick with someone in your family? Your neighborhood? At work? School?

LOREN
Patch it up NOW. TONIGHT! Before you hit the parking lot.

(All three look at the dead bodies, then back to the audience.)

JESSIE
Remember...

ALL THREE STORYTELLERS
Violence'll kill ya.

(All three wave to the audience.)

ALL STORYTELLERS
Good night!!!!

THE END

PROPS

collapsible knives
6-8 swords
2 huge swords
scroll with names
party decorations
3 masks
glitter
2 decorative ladders
2 medicine vials
letter
pen

DIRECTOR'S NOTES

DIRECTOR'S NOTES

DIRECTOR'S NOTES

DIRECTOR'S NOTES